44 Hours
that Changed My Life

by

Ronald P. Snider with Linda Snider

RoseDog Books
PITTSBURGH, PENNSYLVANIA 15238

RoseDog Books
585 Alpha Drive
Suite 103
Pittsburgh, PA 15238
Visit our website at *www.rosedogbookstore.com*

ISBN: 979-8-88925-455-3
eISBN: 979-8-88925-955-8

This book is dedicated to my late wife of 58 years,
Linda Snider,
whose contributions have made much of this work possible.

Foreword

Why have I decided to write a book?

With the rise of divorces and single-parent homes in the country today, this endeavor shall try to show an example of a relationship that has grown and prospered over the years. Our marriage is one of which I am particularly proud because it is based on honesty, communication, and true love for my wife, Linda.

This effort has been contemplated over many years and is intended to share our relationship, our struggles, and our victories over the constant threats of invasion from the outside world pressing for separation divorce and defeat of our marriage.

The modern world was always trying to get between us and force us to do our own thing and thus separate us from each other. We are all subject to the forces of the modern world where it has become easier and easier to just quit relationships, where cheating on one's spouse has become accepted and where a job is the most important consideration in our lives. Where success in life is a constant driving force that keeps us apart.

Our story starts in 1971, when were married for seven years. We had a good marriage, having both come from families where divorce had never occurred. We were both the eldest of children in our families. Linda had one brother and I had two siblings.

As the oldest children in our families, we had been the first experiment in our parents' lives and were subject to the experiences our parents had, who had been through the depression as children and WWII as adults. They had struggled with separation during the war while our fathers served in the military.

While our lives were very simple, growing up in the 50s we were expected to be "seen but not heard," as well as being subject to discipline of our parents. Our lives were very much influenced by what our parents had experienced in their youth. We both came from Jewish families. Our religious observances were somewhat in line with the previous generation. From neither an orthodox home nor non-religious environment, we were brought up to appreciate our heritage, which said to fear God. We were taught to appreciate his presence in our home and in our lives. I grew up as a Reform Jew and Linda was brought up in a more conservative environment.

At the time I was working as a group sales representative with Connecticut General Life Insurance Company in NYC, Linda was an elementary schoolteacher in Fairlawn, NJ. We had been married seven years and were still in the youth of our marriage. We were happy as a couple but influenced by the forces of the modern world, where advancement of our career was the most important force in our lives.

One day a coworker of mine, who had become a particularly good friend, came into the office and asked me to give him $10.00. When I asked what for, he said he was not going tell me but just to trust him that it would be well spent. I did, and then found out he had made a reservation for us to attend a Marriage Encounter Weekend.

Linda and I had never heard of Marriage Encounter and were skeptical of what the experience might be. We had heard of experiences like EST Weekends and were not sure we would attend. Tom again asked us to trust him and please go with an open mind. He said the weekend was designed to make a good marriage better. We did, and we have been blessed ever since.

Chapter 1
Our Introduction to Marriage Encounter

*L*inda and I were introduced to Marriage Encounter by one of my co-workers in New York in 1972.

We had been married for seven years and like most couples we led a normal life. Linda was a stay-at-home mom and I was commuting and working in NYC. We had purchased our home in Paramus, NJ, in 1971. We had two children, a boy aged five and a girl aged two. Our lives revolved around our jobs and home.

We were married in the true sense of the word, but each of us had our own agenda. Linda was the mom, a homemaker concerned with the kids, education, wellbeing of our family. I was the breadwinner concerned with my job, my business career, and things outside our home.

We were not particularly religious, though we were both Jewish. We did not follow all the customs of our religion but knew our religious history and attended services for the high holidays. We left adherence to traditional celebrations to our parents.

We were both the oldest child in our respective families and were the first married as well.

Our friends Tom and Sandy had one day insisted we give him $10.00, which I later found out was for a reservation for a Marriage Encounter Weekend, which they had experienced and were overly excited about. My first reaction was to reject the idea, but since we were awfully close friends, worked for the same company, and had traveled together many times, we agreed and decided to go forward.

Linda was looking forward to the experience, but I was not sure. We arranged for a babysitter for the children and set out on Friday 8/25/72 to the Villa Marie Claire, a Catholic retreat house in Saddle River, New Jersey. We were told to bring snacks for the sharing table, and additionally we were instructed to forget the outside world for the next two days.

Upon arrival we were assigned to our room and asked to assemble in the conference room for introductions. My initial impression of the retreat house was negative. A room with a no decorations except a cross on the wall was foreign to me, who had been brought up in a Jewish home, where my mother lit candles on Shabbat and had kept a kosher home. While we did not adhere to tradition as strictly as my parents, the place was still strange to me personally.

In the conference room we were introduced to three couples and a priest who were going to lead the weekend. The room was adorned with banners extoling the Marriage Encounter Experience. One banner I remember was "God is Love."

We assembled and the couples asked us to introduce ourselves and share our spouses' most endearing qualities. Everyone then shared their spouses' names and endearing qualities. This felt a little strange because I never expected this question. I thought I was smart by giving Linda's most endearing quality as a wonderful homemaker. Later, I came to realize this quality was a description of what she did, not of who she was. Linda's most endearing qualities far exceed her homemaking.

The team couple then introduced themselves, first name only. They explained the essence of the weekend where we would meet in the room, listen to a presentation, and then be asked to write a response, which we would share and discuss with our spouse in the privacy of our room. We were also asked to remove our watches, not discuss our careers or private life with the other couples for the balance of the weekend. After the presentation we were given questions to answer and to write in our blue notebook.

The first question that was asked of us was:

WHY DID I COME HERE TODAY AND WHAT DO I HOPE TO GAIN?

Linda partially responded, "I was really hoping for a more profound question. I wanted to come here because I consider Tom and Sandy sharp people and they were so turned on by it that I thought it had to be good. It seemed to help them understand each other more. I think that we have an excellent marriage and I'm all for everything that will strengthen our marriage and family."

I responded, "The basic reason why decided to come here was because Tom and Sandy had sold my wife so well on the idea of Marriage Encounter. Quite frankly, though, this was a very Catholic-oriented experience. My second reason, therefore, was to make my wife happy. The third reason I came was because we had been fighting so much and I realized that people with closed minds do not learn much."

In addition, in my answer to the first question I included an attack on my spouse for forcing me to come to this weekend. I wrote that she was easily influenced by other people and what they said to her. It was definitely written with a closed mind and illustrated my rejection of her feelings.

We separated and, in our room, read each other's answers. Based on the poor attitude I displayed, we almost got into a fight.

This unfortunately was a symptom we frequently experienced in our marriage to that point. Relying only on prior experience with our parents, we had no better information with which to work. My parents had been strict disciplinarians and had brought me up to listen and not respond. When I had a problem as a child, my dad would tell me to go bang a nail into a piece of wood to ease my frustrations. They offered little more in the way counseling. So after our first encounter on the weekend, I was ready to throw it to the wind.

As you can see, we were miles apart on even going to and experiencing this weekend. I was negative, closeminded, and only there to satisfy my wife's wishes. Linda, on the other hand, was incredibly positive. I had cancelled our first scheduled Marriage Encounter resisting this experience. Like many couples we were far apart in our relationship and communication. We were totally involved in the outside world and failed to put our spouse first.

Our first exchange of letters was not a wonderful experience. Linda read my letter and was upset with what I said. I read hers and realized there was a great deal more to learn that what I thought I knew.

Following the first presentation, still on Friday night, we were instructed to consider only feelings in our discussions, we were asked to express our feeling in the form of a love letter to each other.

The concept of Reflection (writing) and Dialogue (speaking to each other in the privacy of our room) was explained. We were then given a list to illustrate what feelings were so we could adopt and understand how to express them. The team couple explained that feelings are not right or wrong; they just are. We were instructed to describe what a feeling feels like, using illustrations that physically are present, so our partner can relate to the feeling in a physical way. We were told to describe the feeling in a loving way and were given a list to consider.

Some typical feelings ARE:

Hurt
Angry
Joy
Happy
Sad
Confused
Frustrated
Resentful
Jealous, and
Fearful.

After this presentation we were asked to write another reflection responding to the questions:

What are my feelings about what I find most attractive in you?

What are my feelings about what I like best in me?

What are my feelings about what I find most attractive in us?

At this point, and with this writing, I realized this experience was worthwhile and began to change my attitude. I realized we were both adults, with a good life, and the experience might make our lives better.

Over the course of the weekend, we experienced a wonderful closeness we had never experienced before. (We will explain more later.) This weekend flew by and by Sunday night we were elated, excited, and feeling blessed that we had chosen to come on this weekend. We received letters from many couples we did not know, saying they were praying for the success of our weekend. We were both so elated that we didn't want the weekend to end.

As we left the retreat house, we literally floated to the car for the drive home. Smiles on our faces and tears in our eyes, we somehow found or way back to the world from which we came.

The weekend had really succeeded in changing our attitudes toward each other. We were filled with love for the world and anyone in it.

After the weekend, we found out that four couples on our Encounter Weekend had been asked to become team couples. We both were so excited about the experience and thought we wanted to give back some of the joy that we had received. But then were told we could not become part of a team because we were not Catholic. Marriage Encounter was a "Catholic Experience."

When I found this out, I was devastated. We had gained so much from the weekend that I wanted to share it with others. We saw ourselves like the other couples, yet we could not qualify.

At that time, a non-Catholic Expression of Marriage Encounter was just a dream.

Chapter 2
Learning Who We Were

After our Encounter Weekend, we were concerned about how we could keep the feelings of closeness and love we had experienced during the Encounter. We left the weekend with the greatest euphoric feelings and exuberance anyone could imagine. We had left the weekend so high on love we floated home.

Once at home, we thought about our experience and realized that the feelings we discovered on the weekend had to be maintained. This is very hard to do because we had to return to our children, our jobs and the "Modern World." For many couples this is impossible to do. Many of us are incredibly involved in our daily lives and individual activities. We thought about it and decided to change our focus and try to maintain the weekend feelings.

We were welcomed by a community of other encountered couples, who were just as enthusiastic as we were. We joined image groups, rap groups, community Marriage Encounter functions, renewals, and became hosts for other Encounter Weekends. We continued to follow what we were taught on the weekend for our personal communication. The concept of reflection and dialogue, called the daily "10&10," became ingrained in our lives. Our dialogue followed many paths, with questions like, what are my feelings about our home life? What are our feelings about God in our life? How do I feel about being part of a couple?

From the time we first encountered each other as a couple, and for the next months, we did not miss a night of choosing a question, writing a love letter (reflection), and getting together, then sharing (dialogue) about our feelings.

We realized that while we were trying to follow the structure of the weekend, we needed outside influences to guide us and provide a format and audience for us to share our struggle. Our Marriage Encounter community fulfilled that for us, meeting with other couples who thought and felt the way we did. This allowed us to be able to share our stories and issues with friends who listened with their hearts and not with their minds. As part of a community we were accepted and encouraged to share ourselves, which created only more openness and understanding. We also learned a lot about the other couples in our community, as well as their commitment to God. We attended more masses in our first year after the original weekend than we did services in our own Synagogue.

Over the next few months, the continued dialogue and sharing along with occasional disagreements and fights led us to a permanent change in our marriage. We truly fell back in love, but on a much deeper level. Giving of oneself to their spouse became easy and much less an issue as it had once been.

Deciding to love Linda every day changed everything. We continued to reflect on our lives and were successful in creating a kinship that was rewarding and joyful.

Like other Encounter couples, we saw the difference between others in their reactions to each other. Our community was aglow with joy, happiness, understanding, and empathy. Our dialogue became even deeper, and we were even able to achieve unity through the expression of feelings to each other.

Some of our dialogue questions included:

What do you feel when you look at our wedding album? What are my feelings about getting old? Do I accept you as you really are? What are my feelings about Marriage Encounter? and What are my feelings about God in our relationship? I responded to that question as follows:

> *"My feelings about God as it relates to our religion is blah. I feel skeptical about organized religion such a Judaism, Catholicism and Protestant because they are all outward shells for the same God.*
>
> *"I feel upset at our expression of God because we were taught to fear God's power, but not taught to see his gentleness and love."*

Linda's was equally skeptical. She could not relate to God as a Loving God; we were both hung up with the concept of God as part of the Jewish religion. God represented tradition, responsibility, and obligations. We grew closer each time we did our "10&10."

Becoming a Team

One evening toward the end of 1972, we were contacted by a couple named Joe and Diene and asked if we would consider attending a weekend of team training for the establishment of a Jewish Expression of Marriage Encounter. Linda and I discussed the idea and thought about what the original weekend had done for us and whether we were equipped to consider this request. We dialogued about our feelings about Judaism and how it would fit in the weekend and if we were qualified to share our experiences with other couples. We had serious doubts about how religion fit into our lives; we were not particularly religious and certainly not very observant of traditions and practices as many of the other Jewish couples we had met with and whom we had interacted. We agreed God is in our lives, in our home, and in our hearts. The connection between Temple or Synagogue was counter to our feelings. Organized religion was structure, tradition, mysticism, and rules we simply did not want to follow.

On our original weekend, we both felt touched by the Lord in the form of our communication with each other. God as described in the Old Testament, or the Torah, was the furthest from our personal feelings. We saw our marriage as something like a Sacramental gift we were blessed to have. That night we chose a question: What are my feelings about becoming a team couple?

My response was "*I really feel good about Marriage Encounter. Being a team in the Jewish movement will still allow us to keep our current friends and will allow us to expand our horizons. I feel enlightened by what Marriage Encounter has taught me, and we are so lucky to be able to share our feelings with each other. We should try to pass this on to others.*"

Becoming a team couple meant exposing our feelings to others and describing them in the form of the presentations given on the weekends. We did not feel as pure as the couples who gave of themselves and shared their lives with us. We asked questions for our 10&10 (reflection and dialogue) like "WAMF" (What are my feelings?) about God in our relationship.

Linda: "*I am fearful that many of the things I am writing are Judgments. I do not feel God's presence in Judaism, at weddings and funerals. I do not believe we are the chosen people and are any better than anyone else. I can feel God's presence in some people, and not in others. I feel his presence in you, our children and Andy (our weekend Priest).*"

I responded to that question as follows: "*My feelings about God as it relates to our religion is blah, I feel skeptical about organized religion such as Judaism, Catholicism, and Protestantism because they are all outward shells for the same God.*

"*I feel upset at our expression of God because we are taught to fear God's power, but not taught to see his gentleness and love. Before we could go further with our commitment, to becoming a team couple, we should give serious thought to how we fit into our religious beliefs and determine if we could share those feelings with other couples.*"

After a great deal of sharing with our local community, and especially with Jim and Loretta, our closest friends who were also a Catholic team and very committed, we were convinced to go forth and attend a Team Training Weekend.

In January 1973, along with twenty-three other couples Linda and I attended a Team Training Weekend in Cranford, NJ.

The training was run by two couples and a Rabbi and his wife. Unlike our first weekend, this was in a motel, not a retreat house; there was no priest, and the concept of the blessed Sacrament was not there. On our original weekend, the priest spoke of his love for God and marriage to the Church. The couples on this weekend had all made their first encounter within the Catholic faith and were being charged with the responsibility to create a weekend around the Jewish faith. The presenting couples had the same responsibilities, but the Rabbi had to encounter with his spouse, as well as intermesh with his education in Judaism.

The weekend was going to use the same format as before, but it was really going to be different. Instead of the usual question and personal reflections, we were asked questions like:

Why do I want us to become a team?
What do I hope to gain?
What am I willing to sacrifice?
How do I feel about myself tonight?
How do you make me feel about myself tonight?

We both reflected on these questions and quite frankly were surprised by our answers. We did not feel as excited about the other couples on this weekend, because they were undisciplined and talked a lot.

We did not know any of the other couples in attendance, while they all knew each other from Long Island. We frankly felt like fish out of water.

We judged them as not being profoundly serious about the whole thing. However, as the weekend progressed we concentrated on ourselves and responded to the other questions to see if we were serious about this commitment.

I would like to share one of the reflections I wrote on this weekend:

"MY dearest Linda,

"As strongly as you felt about our ten & ten. That is how strongly I feel about carrying Marriage Encounter on.

My idea is threefold, first for our children, they are in their formative years and our love for each other means a lot to them. Secondly, we should spread our love to our family and friends. They will see what love can do and what it has done for us. Finally, and most important I would like to make a commitment to our religion. It is so fortunate we were open enough to come on this weekend., we have done a wonderful thing for ourselves let us spread it to the people of our faith and let us help show them the love we found. Work with me and we will always be close as we are today.

 Love always,

 Ron"

Linda's feelings about the Jewish Expression were quite different than mine. She had no yearning to bring it to the Jewish people. She felt apprehensive about the Jewish Expression and did not see the need for it. She added, "We had been on a beautiful Catholic weekend and welcomed back to a beautiful Catholic community. I never felt any strong need for Judaism before Encounter and do not feel it now. I felt welcomed loved and accepted in our community and am concerned that starting a Jewish Expression would cause a split and have hard feelings. I think that one of the reasons I went along with it is because I wanted to become a team and the Catholic Expression would not accept us. I then thought of the Jewish Expression as something to be there for couples who had difficulty getting along with or understanding Christians."

Our team training weekend was a deep, disturbing experience for both Linda and me. Like Linda, I did a great deal of judging that weekend. I also feared the rumor that only 12 of the 24 couples on the weekend would make it. We shared something in almost every talk. We struggled and judged and even fought until the presentation on Confidence and Dialogue when we finally got ourselves together. We left the weekend on another temporary high. We were a team when Joe told us to take out the list of couples on the weekend and cross out the word "training," leaving only the words "Team List."

We were now a team. We had all the privileges and wore a special label. The impact of the weekend really did not hit us until two months after the actual weekend. Our awareness of our Judaism started to come alive as the message of "be the fullest of who you are" came through to us. The awareness of our Judaism grew as had our awareness of God on our original weekend. We could feel ourselves grow as we committed ourselves to each other, our dialogue, our religion, and our Jewish Encounter family.

Chapter 3
Our Rookie Weekend

About eight weeks after our training weekend, we received a call with our first assignment. Little did we know that our first 44-hour ego trip would require at least 44 hours of preparation and more fights than we had ever experienced in all the years we were married.

As Linda stated in one of our talks, preparing for our first weekend was a horror. We were contacted in the beginning of March and asked to prepare for a weekend on Memorial Day. The next day we were called again and told the weekend was rescheduled for April.

As part of a team in April 1973, the central part the Jewish Encounter community was then located in Long Island, NY. Our first team was made up of Bart and Jane, Bobbi and Ken, Marty and Elaine, all from Nassau County, NY. We found out we were obligated to attend three team meetings before the weekend. The object was for all of us to be comfortable with the presentations we were preparing for the weekend. We had to write and read aloud the presentations to the balance of the team.

We were expected to receive comments, criticism, and praise for our presentations. We got a lot of comments and criticism!

Our first experience with a team meeting was interesting. Here we were meeting three couples for the first time and having to build an instant relationship with them so we could share our feelings, thoughts, and written words. We were expected to accept the criticism openly and without reaction or rejection. This was a very tough assignment. The lead team, Bobbi and Ken, really tried to be all we needed. Even with their openness, we felt a little out of place sharing our presentations accepting their critique and having to rewrite their suggestions.

The team meetings were always in Long Island, and we found ourselves traveling back and forth all the time. In addition to writing talks, we were given other responsibilities for the success of the weekend. We were not alone, but we still had to stick to a set schedule, maintain the strict discipline of the weekend, be available if a couple wanted to speak to us, and maintain the sharing table.

We also all had the responsibility of making the weekend encounter a success for our relationship by participating in all aspects of the weekend, including our own personal encounter. As part of the team, we had to make as much of the weekend for ourselves as possible.

Our first weekend as part of a team was a wonderful experience. Jewish Encounter Weekends started on Saturday night after sundown. The weekend started with a Havdalah service (end of Sabbath) and continued through Monday late afternoon. We were amazed to see forty-eight people come together and 24 couples leave on Monday.

The weekend had a set pattern that is followed by all religions. The first thing we were asked was to introduce ourselves and share our spouse's most endearing quality. The balance of the presentation was further explanations by the rabbinic couple sharing how they felt seeing the blank book on their chair. They explained that Marriage Encounter is a crash course in a technique of communication that you can continue for the rest of your life.

Next, we explained the pattern of the weekend, presentation, question, reflection, and dialogue.

We shared that correcting grammar of spelling in your spouse's reflection was unnecessary and a distraction.

The presenting couple then shared their reaction when asked to write in the notebook why they decided to write and other reasons why the notebook makes sense. The discipline of the weekend came next; silence is to be always observed, and why it is so important. Coffee and snacks are only available before presentation or at a set time. No corrections of grammar or comments when sharing our reflection with your spouse. The next presentation was a nuts-and-bolts presentation given by the administrative team couple (the most senior and in charge of the weekend). Bobbi and Ken told the couples, "This weekend was a friendless, childless, jobless experience." The couples were instructed to leave their phones and watches in their rooms and try to leave the world behind until the weekend was over.

They were briefly given the scope of the weekend, told it was between the husband and wife in private and not to be discussed with others. They were asked to answer and share the following:

Why did I come here? What do I hope to gain?

During this weekend, Linda's and my first as part of a team, we both shared positive thoughts about giving of ourselves. We were feeling elated but also feeling concerned that the split between the Catholic Encounter and the Jewish Encounter would cause a split in our community. We were very gratified by the Catholic couples who greeted all the weekend guests and for their assistance in getting the weekend underway. We loved the idea of sharing ourselves and looked forward to the balance of the weekend.

The second presentation on Saturday night is called orientation and focus, and another part of the team and the religious couple made this presentation. They explained why they decided to write, how it helped getting feelings on paper. They shared their personal difficulties in getting to feelings.

The presenting members of the team then shared how to dialogue:

Read the letter twice without comments or reaction if possible. Reach out toward one another; try to find the person behind the words. Trust of each other was the most important part of the weekend.

They shared their fear of failure. Failure causes us to protect ourselves. They encouraged to not let fear spoil their experience. The couples were all asked to come here because they had good marriages; many of them were sent on the weekend because they have the best marriages. A good marriage does not make the weekend work; it's your feelings that do it.

The experience starts out with a look at us and what we hope to gain from the experience.

They were briefly given the scope of the weekend:

Self
Couple
God
God and Community

They were told it was between the husband and wife in private and not to be discussed with others. We asked them to share their reaction with each other.

The Rabbinic couple then stressed masculinity and how men have a more challenging time writing because being a macho person prevents men from showing their emotions and giving their all. They stressed that the women being especially compassionate often have acceptance of the reflection.

The team couple then explained the concept of open-ended dialogue and reemphasized silence and were told it was between the husband and wife in private and not to be discussed with others. We asked them to write and share our reaction to the following questions:

The men remained in the room and the wives left to their individual rooms.

The final question for the night was:

What is the quality in you I like best?
What is the quality I like in me best?
What is the quality in us that I like best?
How do these qualities make me feel?

We completed the weekend and had a wonderful experience. Our first weekend, our rookie weekend, went off like clockwork. W experienced a wonderful encounter, fell in love with the couples on the weekend, and realized we had much to give and much to receive. After our first weekend we were asked to become an administrative couple and to head up teams for other Encounter Weekends.

We had to write all the talks for the weekend and truly commit ourselves to be a growing part of the encounter experience.

In the following pages, I will endeavor to explain each of the presentations on the weekend, its place in the structure of the weekend, and the dialogue purpose as well as sharing some of the experiences we enjoyed. We were fortunate to share our love on twenty-two Encounter Weekends.

Chapter 4
The "I" Phase of the Weekend

Encounter with Self

The purpose of this talk was to get the couples individually, and honestly, and sincerely to really face themselves as they are and to begin to recognize that there is essential goodness within them. The dialogue purpose is to get them to write in their notebooks, not to be revealed to anyone but just to examine how they can get their deep feelings out on paper. All of the Encounter Weekend is dependent upon a good encounter with self. It is the "I" part of the weekend. Without being able to honestly look at yourself, it is difficult if not impossible to share feelings with someone else. Self-reflections are often the most important part of the weekend.

The following morning the couples on the weekend were awakened and offered the opportunity to participate in morning prayers. Not many people joined us at this time.

After breakfast, where we again stressed no watches, no conversation about jobs and children, and encouraged concentration on the weekend experience, we then assembled in the conference room and introduced the concept of encounter with self. We were asked to list our defects and virtues.

On our original weekend, Linda listed emotional, sensitive, short temper, and very rare feeling physically attractive as defects. For virtues she listed love husband and children, willing to give to them, capable, informed, and admit to mistakes.

My list only had one virtue: good provider. I listed many defects like selfish toward individual property, do not like being part of the group, inadequacy, inferiority complex, and bragging about position.

To show how we change and yet stay the same on our rookie weekend, Linda wrote:

Good points:
Intelligent
Capable
Organized

Bad points:
Selfish
Unloving
Rigid
Intolerant.

I wrote my good points as:
Lover
Generous
Helpful
Kind
Good administrator.

My bad points included:
Spendthrift
Looks for glory.
Braggard
Not open to Linda or kids
And scared, right now.

There was quite a change from our original weekend to our first team weekend. It had been a period of about two years.

The presenting couple introduced the concept of the masks we wear as to how we present ourselves to the world. We shared our personal inadequacy and fears of rejection, thus explaining why we wear masks to identify ourselves. We explained there would be no sharing after this presentation and suggested that the couples jot down notes as they are enlightened by something we said. We asked the couples to be honest with themselves and let their true feelings come to the surface. This is the "I phase" of the weekend, and we want them to consider themselves alone at this time.

We then shared some of the typical masks people wear to help the couples identify the masks they wear in everyday life.

Some typical masks we wear are:

The mask of the perfect marriage: We all were sent here because someone thought we had a good marriage. This mask can interfere with your ability to get into the weekend and keep you from having the best experience.

The mask of openness: Some of us think we are incredibly open and nonjudgmental. We claim to never hide our feelings. However, no one is 100% open, and we all have secrets and fears.

The mask of objectivity. This mask is displayed by the person who says this technique is for those who really need it.

The mask of motherhood is the typical self-sacrificing mother. It appears in a person who whenever the needs of the children are disclosed as they come before her own needs or the needs the spouse.

The mask of the job: Men especially wear this mask. The job comes first, ahead of the children, and family and especially the spouse.

Finally, the mask of the comic. This person is present on many Encounter Weekends. There is always a comment or a joke. Failure to see yourself makes this coverup of a frown with laughter.

On our original Encounter Weekend, I wore the mask of independence. I considered myself an independent individual hardly influenced by the outside world. I also added the mask of the do-gooder willing to help others, lending tools that covered my feelings of inadequacy.

I wore the mask of position, which was useful in seeing our place in life and expecting others to achieve the same level of success.

On our original weekend, Linda shared her masks as the mask of not caring, because she was afraid of being rejected. She also said she was tired of being put upon all the time. The other mask she wrote was the mask of being capable.

On our rookie weekend, Linda shared: *"I really feel confused about the way I feel about myself today. Sometimes I feel selfish and then I feel badly about feeling selfish, I know I have the Quality of being able to manipulate people. I seem to be able to outsmart them. It is great for me, but it makes me unfaithful to people I've outsmarted. I feel good when someone loves me."*

I wrote: *"About my masks, I sometimes wonder if I haven't found my core mask and if there is still another one under the one, I just described the feelings I have about myself are as a generous slob at times although they have changed a lot since August, I can't understand how I Act as I do sometimes.*

"I think it's because I want power or prestige. If I am a biggie with Linda, people will like and accept me more. I still feel badly about myself as a person and still feel very inadequate. I wonder about my ability to cope with problems and my ability to be a total success."

We shared our feeling about compliments, how do compliments affect us and how do they make us feel.

Linda shared: *"When someone compliments on my personal appearance. I feel embarrassed. I can never say thank you graciously, but always make an excuse that it's an old outfit or it only cost a few bucks. If someone says I've lost weight, which is the nicest compliment I can get, I answer I still must lose more.*

"If someone compliments me on how I keep my home, I am extremely grateful, I pride myself on being capable of running a household and I am grateful if someone recognizes it. I usually say a meek thank you but am thinking if you only really knew the real me."

I shared: *"Compliments to me always represent a challenge. I love to receive them, but I really am a poor recipient of them. It seems that whenever I receive a compliment I must deny or knock it. If the compliment is about how I look, my response is no, I haven't lost weight, or you've seen this suit before. Most of the time I really don't feel worth of a compliment, I rarely received them as a child and to a point have learned to live without them.*

"At this point in the weekend, we talked about B'zelem Elohim (image of God) we were told that God doesn't make Junk and because we were made in God's image, we are basically good people. When I first heard the expression 'God Doesn't make Junk' on our original weekend, I thought it was silly. I thought it was the presenting couple trying to use this concept to build confidence in myself. The words had no meaning to me.

"Now, however, on this our rookie weekend, I feel comforted and soothed, I know I was made by God and God doesn't make Junk. I feel reassured, whole, and important. The expression reminds us we are all God's children, created in his image and there is something of worth and value in everything we do."

We then asked the couples to observe the discipline of the weekend once again, to write in their books for the full time, to dig deep into themselves, and to return to the conference room when the allotted time is over.

The question we asked was:

"What are my good points? What are my bad points? What masks do I wear that cause me to behave as I do? How do I really feel about myself?"

After an allotted period for writing, we asked the couples to return to the conference room and assemble for the next presentation. We all tried to maintain the discipline of the weekend, discouraging talk among the couples. The group had not exchanged books or discussed their last writings. We thanked them for their attention so far and complimented them on being able to put their thoughts on paper.

Chapter 5
The "We" Phase of the Weekend

Marriage in the Modern World
The general purpose of this talk is to define that their lifestyle is established not only by actions but a personal way of living and a way of life. We want them to recognize that the husband and wife can encounter each other with awe. We help them realize there is a pattern to their marriage.

We want them to get to see that the world has a definite plan for their marriage. The basis of the plan is to live as married singles. We also want them to realize their marriage is intimate but not private. Everyone has a stake in our marriage. Another objective is to get across the idea that love is not just a feeling, but a decision. This is really the core-content talk of Marriage Encounter. The dialogue purpose is to take personal reflection out of the I phase and to the we phase of the weekend. It's their first opportunity to write their personal feelings on paper to their beloved in the form of a love letter, and to communicate lovingly with their spouse.

We introduced the next presentation and explained to the couples that this section of the weekend is part of the we phase of the weekend. The first presentation is called "Marriage in the Modern World." We all shared the fact that we were never really trained to be married while in fact we were all trained by our parents and friends to be private and possessive. Everyone has their own outlets and interests. We were taught to respect each other's privacy and that each of us must live up to our own potential. Many of us believe we are entitled to do our own thing, "when you work hard you deserve time alone as a reward." Men and women are not different; they all take personal responsibility for their individuality. This is called "The World's Plan for our marriage." We are all supposed to be married singles.

Is this the only way? What about God's plan? We explained that each of us makes our own contribution to our marriage in our own way.

Everyone has a stake in each other's marriage. We compare ourselves to others around us and judge ourselves by those standards.

Linda shared she was never trained to be married. "I felt unprepared and inadequate for marriage but later realized that I had been trained for marriage by my parents, aunts, and uncles, and above all our peers. I also learned a lot about marriage from movies, novels, radio, and TV. All our lives we been influenced by what the world thinks a marriage should be. And without knowing it, our attitudes toward marriage were formed. A marriage is a partnership where each partner performs his own function. The man is the breadwinner, and the wife is the housekeeper; however, I was never crazy about housework and did enjoy getting out and working a couple of days of the week. Every time I wanted to get a bit of part-time work was made to feel guilty. The idea of marriage was to settle down, accept our individual roles, and have no further challenge."

Like Linda, I had no formal training to be married. I was twenty when I married and had just finished school. I looked back on my education and even courses in psychology and human relations that never mentioned how I should act or what marriage meant. It is scary when you think of it, because marriage is one of the biggest steps you'll ever take and yet we have no training for it. Many of my attitudes toward marriage came from tall tales and folklore I had heard. They included: Wives should never know about finances; tell her when you get a raise, keep the bills paid, but do not tell her where it comes from.

A wife's place is in the home, specifically in the kitchen and more importantly in the bedroom. Our marriage is built on family. l wasn't sure I wanted to give up being as son when I got married. After we were married, we found ourselves communicating less and less on the same topics, we progressed up the ladder of life, from apartment to apartment to a house, from no children to the birth of our son, then our daughter. We fell into the world's plan for our marriage. We were married singles.

Some of the typical expressions of married singles were a night out with the boys, a mahjong game for the girls, a hobby that takes us away from our spouse, working in the garage, or watching TV by yourself. All these contribute to being separate and aloof from the other.

Why does this happen?

Well, there are three stages of love that we all share: The first is romance, when we can't get enough of each other, our first date, our first kiss, considering yourself totally open with each other, loving the qualities you see in each other.

The second stage is disillusionment. "She is not who I thought she would be." Marriage is not what I thought it would be and the disappointment when you realize that to be so.

But how do we get past this stage and what can we do to improve our marriage? The answer is having a set of rules for dialogue and a set of rules for fighting. Being able to communicate with each other is a wonderous thing that will lead to the third state of marriage: "True Joy."

"True joy," Linda said, "is when Ron and I are awfully close to each other, I feel peaceful and content. It is like a protected sort of feeling like all's well and nothing can hurt me."

I added, "True joy for me is those few fleeting moments when we are one in mind and spirit. They can take place anywhere and anytime, but when they occur know that what I have done for us has been right. True joy can only be achieved when I make a conscious decision to love and give 100% of myself to Linda." Love is a decision.

The couples were then introduced to the concept of "A decision to love."

Linda shared on our original weekend: "When the couple giving this talk told us that love is a decision, it went completely over my head and did not make any sense at all. In fact, later at one of the meals, a girl asked me how I felt when I first heard love is a decision. I was embarrassed to tell her thought they were wrong. How could love be a decision?

"When I first saw Ron, I did not say, why don't you make the decision to love that guy? My heart did flipflops, and my palms got all sweaty. My pulse rate went higher. It was not a decision; it was an emotion."

I could understand the words intellectually, but I was confused about the meaning in a practical sense. Sometimes I react to things in a slow plotting way. When I first met Linda, it only took me a few months to ask her for as date. To me, falling in love was a slow building process and when I finally asked her out I was quite sure of my intentions.

In thinking back to when I first made a decision to love, I must go back to the period of disillusionment in our marriage. I could have chucked the whole thing but instead looked at Linda through the same eyes as when we met. Today I try to make the decision to love every day. A decision to love is a decision to put your spouse first and give 100% to your relationship. It is putting selfish feelings aside and giving 100% of yourself every day. Rather than a 50/50 relationship, a decision to love is for each of us to strive for giving 100% to our relationship.

In the dialogue, we were told to be honest with our feelings and be willing to be totally open. We were told not to be afraid, not to question the feelings you are writing, not to write what you think your spouse wants to hear. Keep your spouse in mind as you write. Picture your spouse when you write a love letter. Do not use abbreviation or outlines. Be humble and willing to open up. Share your book gently and accept what you read. Read the reflection twice. Hold hands when you read each other's love letter, and start with a kiss.

Linda said, "I always take a few moments before I write to picture him in my mind. I usually start the love letter with 'Dearest Ron' and use frequent endearments. *I always write with my love for him showing because it is much easier to tell him how I feel if I always tell him I love him at the same time.*"

The rabbinic couple emphasized that "unhealthy disagreements lead to lasting resentments."

We subsequently gave the couples a handout called "Symptoms of Spiritual Divorce" and asked them to check all the symptoms that applied. We explained that checking too few symptoms meant they were not being totally honest. We encouraged them to dig deep into their hearts so they could identify every symptom.

The list included:

1. Prolonged unhappiness or sadness in our marriage.
2. Mutual coldness or indifference.
3. Frequent tension, fearfulness, bad temper, or arguments.
4. Insults and rudeness.
5. Holding each other up for ridicule.
6. Teasing beyond my or your tolerance for humor.
7. No intimate communication and fear of being open and honest.
8. A feeling of being alone, insecure, misunderstood, or avoided.
9. Atmosphere of insincerity, and distrust.
10. More confidence in a third person than in your spouse.
11. Avoiding situations that need attention and failure to plan together.
12. Lack of concern for the other's interests or problems.
13. Continuous escapes—such as liquor, drugs, work, sports, shopping, TV, etc.
14. Personal activities that cause conflict (nights out, sports, use of internet, etc.).
15. Attitude of selfishness or self-centered demands on our marriage.
16. Avoiding or refusing sexual relations.
17. Lack of enthusiasm, faith, and hope in our love and in our marriage.
18. Lack of spiritual life or keeping it private from the other.
19. Lack of appreciation for my or your contribution to our marriage.
20. Lack of tenderness, courtesies, gentleness, or respect.
21. Drive for material wealth.

With this list we asked the couples to try and identify all the symptoms that apply but only to write about one or two. Write about the feelings that relate to the symptom, not about the symptom. Write to reveal yourself, not to change your spouse, and above all write lovingly.

We also explained the rules for fighting to the couples and gave them some guidelines. They are as follows:

The rules for fighting:

1. Stay on the subject: If you are fighting about a cup, don't bring the saucer into the act.
2. Keep criticism to yourself.
3. Do not hit below the belt.
4. No past history.
5. Try fighting in the nude!

The couples split up with the men staying in the conference room and the women returning to their respective rooms to answer the question:

"Please share your struggle to make a decision to love and allow your beloved to be who he or she needs to be. Do I see and accept you as you really are and how does it make me feel?"

Areas for Reaching Out

This presentation is the second in the we phase of the weekend. The purpose of this talk is to help the couples begin to find one another through areas that have been closed off or never opened, in a way that focuses on the issue rather than themselves and their relationship. It is to make clear to them that the issue is not the issue; their relationship is. The dialogue purpose is to share the experience around the issue and the struggle to try to get to acceptance. The concept of acceptance is explained as being willing to put aside your feelings and relate to the feelings expressed by your spouse. Acceptance is a step forward toward the commitment to eliminate privacy and reach out to fully belong to one another.

On our original weekend, the team couple explained the stages of feelings. Such as:

1. the "putting up with it" stage,
2. the "passing like ships in the night" stage,
3. the "if I were in your shoes, I would feel the same way" stage,
4. the "I am glad you feel that way" stage,
5. I enjoy your feeling that way.

These are all stages of toleration. Feelings above toleration lead to acceptance. Acceptance is when you can try to feel your spouse's feelings. I accept your feelings and want them to be mine too.

Finally, the last stage is unity, a feeling of oneness.

The question we were given was:

Go down the list of areas for reaching out to one another. Check the areas that have feelings you think your spouse does not understand about you, then put an X on the areas where you have feelings you don't understand in your spouse.

Write a love letter about your feelings. Example, what are my feelings toward death and how do they affect your commitment to living? Or today is your last day on earth, have I lived my life to the fullest and how does my answer make me feel? I am standing at your gravesite, what are my feelings right now?

On our original weekend, I wrote:

"Dearest Linda,

"This assignment is more difficult than the last to me. It is difficult for me to understand and relate to some of the comments regarding death. I believe there are only a few areas in which we have reached out to, as we usually communicate well. The biggest difference between us is our relationship with our relatives. Our upbringing and relationship

with family is so different. I feel so bad about the death of your father, not so because of my loss, but more because of yours. In losing your father, you also lost your mother. It is too bad she can't read this because she might change. I feel sadness when your mother turned on you and made you unhappy. I also feel sad for her because she needs help and is too selfish to realize she can be wrong. This however is not expressing my feelings. I love my parents and forgive them for their faults. In a way I wish you could do the same with your mother. Honey, this reflection is not right so let's try another subject.

"Our sexual relationship is something I feel strongly about and don't know how to express on paper. I feel happy, sad, and frustrated at the same time. I love you so, sometimes I want to just eat you up and other times I just do not want to have you at all. I feel frustrated many times when you turn me off...."

On our original weekend, Linda wrote:

"Hi Honey,

"I feel afraid to write now because I tend to write thoughts more than feelings. You deserve more than that and you're giving me more. I wish I could make you happier sexually. I love you very much and when making love I know you do everything you possibly can to make me happy and responsive. I feel warm and secure as if nothing could hurt me when you're holding me.

"You probably don't know but, I am jealous of your job. I think I resent anything outside of our home that is so important to you, and you've never done anything to make me jealous. I feel happy you enjoy it so much. It's just the idea that a big part of you is away from me.

> *"You know how I feel about my relatives, but sometimes*
> *I feel smothered by your family. I really like them, but I feel*
> *like your mother forces me to be a do-gooder in front of them*
> *for them to accept me. I could not deal with thoughts of your*
> *death (God Forbid). I would like to know more about your*
> *feelings on sexual relations and marriage…"*

This presentation is not to feel each other's feelings but to become predisposed to what the person is revealing. What is most important here is to reach out to your beloved and not so much to the feeling. In addition, we asked the couples to express feelings through non-verbal communications.

Non-verbal is not only intercourse. It is much more, a touch of the hair or a kiss on the cheek are both non-verbal forms of communications.

Openness

After lunch on Sunday, the next presentation is entitled openness.

The general purpose of this talk is to knock down more barriers to dialogue that exist in the couple's relationship. It is to concentrate on privacy in our dialogue that keeps us from sharing our full relationship. The privacy of not being willing to reveal who I truly am or privacy that prevents a person to fully reveal who they are. The dialogue purpose of this talk is to explain and describe the lived experience of reaching for unity by "experiencing with the heart."

On our original Catholic weekend, this talk was entitled *"The Parable."* It is based on the Parable of the Sower, which originated in the New Testament in the book of Matthew.

We were told a story by Andy, our priest:

> *"The Parable of the Sower was told to the crowd that*
> *had gathered around Jesus. Jesus tells the story of a Sower*
> *who scattered seeds on four different types of soil. The first*
> *type of ground was hard, and the seed could not sprout or*

grow at all and became snatched up instantly. The second type of ground was stony. It was able to plant and begin to grow, however, it could not grow deep roots and withered in the sun. The third type of ground was thorny and although the seed could plant and grow, it could not compete with the number of thorns that overtook it. The fourth ground was good soil that allowed the seed to plant deep, grow strong, and produce fruit."

The lesson of this story is: He takes what is sown in him and shares the gospel of the kingdom with others, many coming to faith because of his obedience, as God works through him.

On our original weekend, we both had some difficulty with this talk. Coming from our religious perspective, we were unfamiliar with the New Testament and the quotation from the Book of Matthew. It was foreign to us, although we understood what the concept explained. The question was: How am I selfish to you in not sharing myself and in not listening, and how does it make me feel?

Linda wrote:

"My biggest problem is my laziness and fear of rejection. I guess I didn't give you enough credit in being interested in my inner thoughts and maybe I didn't trust you enough to tell you. Perhaps it was easier not to face them myself. I didn't think you would understand them, and it was just too much trouble to tell you. I feel badly because I sold you short and you understand much more about me than I gave you credit for. You always tried to tell me more of your thoughts than I would tell you mine. I would keep things inside of me and then blame you for not reading my mind. I'm much less afraid to tell you things today than yesterday because I've started to realize how much you do love

*me and the thought that if you disagree with isn't going to
change your opinion of me."*

Linda's realization here is one of acceptance of openness toward me.
On our original weekend I wrote:

> *"This question is a tough one, since I feel I reveal al-
> most everything to you. As for listening, I feel sure I have
> failed in some ways. I have been selfish in not revealing my
> true feelings about religion, sex, and our relationship.*
>
> *"Religion has always been a dark corner for me. I want
> to believe and practice my religion but am afraid it will have
> an adverse effect on my career, so I hide it or negatively
> flaunt it sometimes. I am embarrassed about the Jewish
> image the modern world has, and do not want to be part of
> it. Chasidim (extremely orthodox Jews) turn me off and dis-
> gust me because of what people think of them and con-
> sequently me...."*

In the Jewish Expression of Encounter, we talked about openness and
its opposite, selfishness. We offered the explanation that if we are open to
each other, it is easier to share deep feelings and in respect to ourselves and
God. The Rabbi and his wife shared an appropriate passage dealing with
openness to each other and openness to God.

I remember when I first heard the reading on our original Catholic weekend, I thought it was a religious talk and had nothing to do with us. But I
missed the point. Now I realize that to know oneself, spouse, and God re-
quires that we be open to reveal and listen to your beloved. It is like listening
with your heart and not your head.

I remember that on our original weekend, I shared how I was selfish in
giving of myself. I was not always open and held back feelings that would
make waves. I looked for safe subjects in the list of areas for reaching out to

each other. I looked for subjects that I wanted to discuss with Linda and picked subjects for myself that we had already discussed many times before. I was also selfish reading Linda's reflection. I didn't always dig for Linda's feelings. I let her tell them to me and didn't say "tell me more."

The goal of this talk is to attain openness. The opposite of openness is selfishness. How are we selfish?

We are selfish where we do not keep the discipline, don't write the full time, don't dig for real feelings, and describe them fully. We must ask ourselves, did I dig deeply to disclose feelings? Did I write what I wanted our beloved wants to hear? Did I write how I would like to feel and not how I really felt? Do I share a safer feeling and choose to hide another feeling that would cause pain? Did I hand over my book with defenses down or my guard on alert? Did I make light of the nonverbal or go directly to nonverbal and not talk out the feelings? Did I read my beloved's reflection with my attention on what I had written and not on the words she wrote?

On our original weekend, I really tried to be open and loving and listen to what Linda said with all my heart. But as I looked back on it now, I must wonder if I was really open, or if it was just a role I played in our dialogue. After our original weekend, in the beginning I saw dialogue as a wonderful tool I could use to bring out Linda's feelings to show her they were wrong and make her change them over to my way of thinking. I would write faithfully every day, carefully constructing our question and dominating the dialogue. I listened intently, looking for my opening. Like a hockey player skating back and forth in front of the net waiting for the puck to come my way, waiting for a false move and a chance to score. Since I really didn't reveal too much of myself, I became bored and laid back and looked at the ceiling.

Occasionally we had a breakthrough and would gain some renewed strength. But basically, our dialogue was controlled by my questions and Linda listening. As time went on, I saw myself sharing less and less of myself. We were really astounded at how much regression we found when we took a vacation from home and our dialogue for about two weeks. We went back to being closed like we were before our original weekend. On that trip, we were at each other, thinking angry thoughts and unwilling to share ourselves with each other.

After the trip we went back to dialogue with a whole new attitude, each having something to share with the other. I am as unique as Linda. We each are sometimes right and sometimes wrong. We were then truly open to each other. More recently, our openness to each other seems to run in tandem with us being in relationship. If we are struggling to be for each other, we can share the most difficult feelings about ourselves or each other and accept them. However, when we are not working on our relationship, we are not the least bit open. We tend to find fault with things the other does and not accept the slightest deviation from what we each see as normal.

The goal of openness *is understanding with the heart.* Understanding with the heart is a higher and much more loving way of listening than with the head. Like acceptance, it is much harder to achieve. The effort to achieve this involves being open and honest and also being unselfish with your feelings.

One of the times we reached this level of closeness was when I described the feeling of helpless frustration we faced when we have a disagreement and could not accept each other's apology. To arrive at this acceptance took a number of days of dialogue; at times we both felt like rubber bands being stretched to the breaking point. One night we chose a question: "When I find it hard to *make a decision to love,* how does it make me feel?"

Linda wrote:

> *"When I can't make a decision to love you I feel hurt, rejected, unloved and uncared for, lonely and misunderstood. My feeling of hurt is overwhelming, and I have no control over it. It would be like a baby bird falling out of a tree and breaking a wing and being told to fly. The hurt covers me like a plastic mold over my body and I'm helpless under its weight...."*

I wrote:

"When I find it hard to <u>make a decision to love</u> I feel myself strangling in my own anger and desire for revenge. I feel caught up in my emotions to the point where feel myself gasp for breath. When I can't turn the other cheek, I feel ashamed of myself. I detest myself when I choose not to love you. I feel small and insignificant. I feel out of control almost like I'm being sucked down the drain by the rush of dirty water...."

We realized that until we were able to accept each other, we couldn't be open with each other.

Chapter 6
The "We and God" Phase of the Weekend

Marriage in the Plan of God
This presentation occurs in the afternoon on Sunday at about 4:45 P.M. The couples have returned from the presentation and dialogue on openness, and we are now moving into the next phase of the weekend. We begin to see how we interact with our relationship to God as it relates to our marriage. This talk provides us a detailed description of our attitudes toward each other before Marriage Encounter. The general purpose of the talk is to point out that everybody has a stake in our marriage, and that God has a very definite plan for us in contradiction to the world's plan. The modern world wants us to be married singles and to be private. God's plan is for us to be a couple and belong to one another and strive to fulfill the promise of scripture in Genesis 2:24: "And They shall be as one."

The idea is to strive to create unity in our relationship. Martin Buber, a Jewish philosopher, describes our relationship as not us, but I thou. Meaning I am for my beloved and my beloved is for me. The question for this talk is: Name three specific instances when I felt closest to you. Describe each feeling of closeness in loving detail.

On our original weekend, my reaction when I heard the name of this talk was one of "Oh, well, now I can really relax." It was late in the afternoon, and everyone was kind of worn down from the previous presentations, and I wasn't much interested in things related to God or his plans. I decided to turn myself down and just keep the pot simmering on a low flame. Since then, my reactions have been different. I've realized the importance of this presentation and really try to key in on what it says. When you are tired you really must try harder and give more of yourself to make the encounter a success. The weekend is all inclusive. Missing some parts because your turned off or disinterested will only allow you to partially succeed.

Linda added:

"Before dialogue, my attitude toward Ron was one of inferiority. I saw him as the head of the household, the breadwinner, and the provider. He was just starting out in a demanding but financially rewarding career. I saw his job as very responsible and requiring much more intellect and worldliness than mine at home. I saw his problems and the decisions he had to make as more important and of much greater consequence than the ones I had to make. He was trying to prove himself and build a future for our family. If he had to be away for weeks at a time on a business trip, it was up to me to manage without him.

"One of the things I used to do is bribe Ron. If I thought someone in his family was going to make a demand on us that I wasn't willing to comply with, I would make a special dinner and be especially sweet. If there was a TV program I wanted to see, I would ask him to choose the programs to see before and after so I could see the one, I wanted. Before dialogue, our communication was very often routine and mechanical. Every night when he came home, I would ask how was work never bothering to listen to his reply. If he answered the building burnt down, I would probably say oh how nice dinner will be ready in fifteen minutes ...When we talked, we never really took the time to share ourselves and never had the urgency to really know

who the other person really was. I always tried to prove I was a good person. I always wanted him to be proud of me and be happy that he married me. I tried to be a good house-keeper so Ron would see that I was living up to my end of the bargain.

"Before dialogue, my attitude toward God was one of inferiority. I saw God as the Almighty being up in the sky somewhere. I know that I believed in his existence but wasn't sure he was involved in my everyday life, God had the whole world to worry about and my problems were very small and insignificant in comparison. I used to bribe God, when I was pregnant, I said please let this baby be healthy and I will try to be the best mother. When I thought I might be seriously ill, I asked him to spare me anything serious and I promise I'll never smoke again. If I wanted Ron, to be successful in obtaining a new piece of business I would promise him to put the money we earned to good use.

"My communication with God was also mechanical and routine. I would say my prayers every night without being aware of it. l never gave much thought to what I said in my prayers, and I was never really sure if he heard me or if I was willing to listen to the message he was sending me.

"When I went to Temple on the high holy days, I would point out to God how many hours I stayed. I felt separate and distant from God. Days would go by when I didn't think about him and was sure wasn't He wasn't thinking about me."

I added…

"My attitudes toward Linda were quite different before dialogue than now. Before the weekend, I saw myself as very

much superior and independent of Linda in many ways. I considered myself the breadwinner of the family and believed I had certain rights which I could exercise whenever I wanted to. I saw myself as the head of the family, the decision maker, and the boss. I saw my job as better than hers. I felt annoyed if her job interfered with me and my time. Cleaning the house was fine, as long as it was done between 9 and 5 on Monday through Friday. When Linda asked me to help clean the house on Saturday my feeling was imposed upon. I felt superior in my ability to deal with people. I could get about whatever I wanted in my business life and expected that position to carry forward as home as well. When it came to dealing with people in a business situation, with a merchant or especially in a restaurant I saw Linda as a pushy person who would insist on things being done her way."

While I felt superior and independent in so many areas, at the same time I felt very judged by Linda. I saw her as a better fighter, parent, and economist than me. Whenever we had a disagreement, I saw myself as the loser before we started. I could not allow a disagreement to keep up very long and fought for peace at any price. Though we fought infrequently, when we did I saw myself always in a defensive position. I saw Linda as the judge, and I would try to justify my position weakly because I could not think of enough past examples that could prove my point and knew I was finished before I started. I used to claim Linda had a file card memory and could produce reasons or incidences to prove her point, which I had forgotten.

I also saw myself as less capable than Linda as in our role as parents. She had an unbelievable amount of patience with our children. I had neither the patience or understanding of their needs that were required and, as a result, imposed my values on our children or lost my temper when my standards were not complied with. Linda by comparison could sit with them, cuddle them, and listen to them to make their hurt better.

Before dialogue I felt less capable in managing money than Linda. I would always spend whatever I had and usually a little more... I never let Linda handle family finances because I was fearful she would do a better job than I. When I gave her the house money for the week, I was never concerned because I knew there would be some left over at the end of the month. Whenever we went shopping, she would carefully inspect each item, knew the unit price and how much she paid last week. She frequently shopped for bargains and avoided items that were too expensive.

Before dialogue, I also bribed Linda. Our relationship was one of give and take, yet I always believed a machine works better if it is lubricated. So I treated her in the same fashion. If I wanted to play golf on the weekend, I would offer to help Linda with some of her responsibilities so she'd be free to relax while I played golf.

My attitudes toward God before dialogue were cold, independent, and indifferent. I felt superior and independent from God in many ways. As a child I was forced to attend religious school, Sunday School, Bar Mitzvah classes, and Confirmation class. The day I was confirmed I decided I had had enough of God to last me a lifetime. I cut the umbilical cord between God and myself.

I felt like I had removed a ball and chain from around my leg. Up to that point I had seen God only in terms of work that I was forced to do. For me, there was no realism to God. I looked at the world around me and saw fighting, poverty, hardship, and I judged that I could solve my problems better than God solved his. I went to synagogue to please my parents. When there, I usually counted the pages until the end of the service, frequently taking a break and usually leaving before the service was over. I did not acknowledge his presence in my life. God was in the synagogue, and I was only there very infrequently.

Since we have struggled to improve our communication through dialogue, I no longer do the things I did before. My attitude toward Linda had changed to a great degree. There are still times when we revert to our old ways, but at least I am aware of some of the significant differences in my attitudes toward her. Our original weekend was only the beginning of a period of awakening within me. The daily dialogue, the openness to each other, the understanding of who and what Linda is has really helped. I no longer see Linda's place in our home as inferior to mine. She has an especially prominent place in our lives. Her duties of being a mother to our children, running the house, and keeping our lives in order are just as important as my job and its responsibilities. I realize she has many pressures in her life and needs an outlet for her frustrations as I do. Just as she needs a time to be alone and a time for reflection, her need for earning some money and feeling financially worthwhile is very understandable and worthy of respect. While I would like to say I have totally changed and do the dishes every night and clean house on Saturday, I cannot. It still takes a prod for me to do this consistently, I do see the need to give her a hand and do it not as a bribe or with strings attached. I've have learned to accept the fact that she is an equal in our relationship with her own virtues and defects. We no longer dialogue to change each other but strive to accept each other where we are today.

Since we have engaged in daily dialogue, my attitude toward God has radically changed.

God is no longer a cold, distant, and indifferent. I no longer see God as something to fear as I look at the world around me. I see God as the producer of the movie while man is the director. God orders life while we are responsible for the way we act within God's world. God no longer represents an obligation. Today he is the image of strength that lives in my heart, my home, and is a part of my life. The vision of God from my youth as God to fear has become a God to love. I see God now as a shoulder to lean on, or a source of strength to which I can turn in a time of stress. A loving God who gives me the wherewithal to be who I am. Through understanding his plan for us, I can accept disappointment or rejection as his will. I still cannot touch him but the knowledge that his strength is on my side makes it easier to accept and feel his presence. If I participate in an incident that causes pain or sorrow, I can look back and be thankful it wasn't worse.

Since dialogue, I see my relationship to God as a warm, loving relationship, which includes the warmth of his presence, the gentleness of his touch, the support of his love, and the strength of his wisdom in my home, and a part of my everyday life.

Linda added, *"Since dialogue I no longer feel inferior to Ron. I do not see his job and career as being more than mine. Our constant communication and awareness of each other makes me feel like a greater and more important part of his life. I have a better understanding of his job and what it entails and have even started to help in his office when I am needed. We both see the things that I must cope with at home on a daily basis as being much more important and significant than before. Because of our dialogue, I do not see a need to protect Ron from my little problems anymore. Because of our dialogue, these things have become as real to Ron as they are to me and became as much a part of his life as they are of mine. I no longer need to bribe Ron. The situation just does not come up anymore. We have become aware of each other's feelings that bribery is not necessary. With better communication with each other, we have become truly more interested in each other. I always have a constant awareness of my beloved. I understand many of the problems we each face and have made it easier to express because I realize the intensity that we each share trying to take on the feelings of the other. The time we spend together now is rich and deep and full of love and meaning. Since dialogue, my attitude toward God has changed too. I no longer feel inferior to God. He no longer lives up in the sky. He is within me and my loving relationship with Ron. I no longer feel small and insignificant in God's eyes. I know I am very important to him, and he to me. I feel his presence all the time and most strongly when I am a loving person. I've stopped making promises and asking for special favors I have faith in God and his judgement and no longer need to bribe him to do things my way. Prayer is no longer something I say routinely because I found that when I am closing Ron out of my life, it is very easy to close God out also. When God accepts me in my humanness, he knows I am good and worthy without having to prove it all the time."*

At this time the couples were given the question, were told to separate, write their reflection as a love letter and, upon completion of the allotted time, return to their individual rooms for dialogue.

Confidence and Dialogue

This presentation begins at about 7:30 P.M. on Sunday night. It takes place after dinner, when the couples have had a break from the earlier routine of presentation, writing, and dialogue. Many of the couples are starting to see the results of the day's activities, and there is a definite change in the demeanor of the presentation room. It is quieter, more and more couples are quietly talking to themselves, and not so much inter-couple chatter is present.

The purpose of this talk is to get the couples to lay aside their fears and be open to one another and also to further introduce them to the details of continued dialogue. The objective is to show them that the limitation on their openness comes from their own fears and not the other person. It is to point out that the key to dialogue is confidence and that without confidence there can be no unity and the plan of God goes out the window. It also reinforces the full relationship with commitment to practice the daily 10&10. This talk tries to explain that the weekend is not a one-shot deal but is a commitment to a way of life through daily dialogue.

The purpose of the weekend is reinforced here, explaining that the goal of the weekend is to *recognize who we are, what masks we wear and with acceptance that, understanding with the heart and unity are the goals.*

In this presentation, we emphasize that confidence is the goal of dialogue, not for one's talents or abilities, and also not for garbage dumping or confessions of the past. It is not for advice or consolation. It is for revelation of present feelings. The most important part of this talk is to instill that *Confidence is a decision, a decision to love.*

The rabbinic couple first shares how they felt on their wedding day. They explain that we don't get married just our wedding day, but we marry every day by saying yes to one another. We say yes to each other by doing the daily dialogue. The concept of "Kiddushin" (daily sanctification) is explained and making a decision to love every day is a form of Kiddushin.

The question asked after the talk is "What feeling do I have I find most difficult to share with you? Describe the feeling in full loving detail."

On our original weekend, Linda shared, *"This is tough. I guess it is my feelings of being inadequate sexually and not being able to always please you. I do not share my feelings with you because I do not know what the answer is. I love you and I want to be close to you and express my love physically. I do not think I would be afraid because I feel your love and feel closer to you spiritually than I ever have. I think I am afraid to let our love grow into something so beautiful that it would be much harder to deal with if I ever lost you. You cannot be as hurt if you are not involved. Losing my father and my relationship with my mother has made me want to be less vulnerable in a relationship with someone. Death and rejection really can happen, and they frighten me. I keep my love feelings from you. I am afraid to let you know how much I love because then you will want to make love and I am afraid to let you down. I feel badly about not being a more open and tolerant person. I never realized that honesty and tolerance were qualities until you showed me. I feel badly that I am so concerned about other people's feelings and opinions....*

"It took many, many months of work on both our parts for Ron and me to let this caterpillar become a butterfly. Through dialogue, Ron realizes that my growing does not make him smaller. Now we are two adult mature whole people struggling to grow as individuals and as a couple."

On our original weekend, I wrote: *"I have been asked to tell you what feelings I have about myself which I find most difficult to share with you. The answer to this question is extremely hard for me. I am not sure can put my finger on specific point. I know guilt feelings are difficult to share as are selfish ones.*

"But right now, really cannot think of any bad ones. My persistent feeling of inferiority is something I have tried to discuss but do not believe we have fully. Honey, I love you and do not want you to think less of me for my inability to answer. Right now, after writing that paragraph I feel as if I have let you down terribly. I'm sure I know you are writing, and I am thinking about that instead of my feelings. As I love you more and more, my compassion grows and feel sorry for what you said in the room about not being able

to tell me everything. I cannot get it out of my mind since I love you and need you. I want to share all my feelings with you.

"I just looked back at the list of feelings and in the time that is left I am going to explain my feelings of fear. With your help in dialogue on that subject maybe we can reach a form of unity. Fear is a difficult feeling for me. Fear of job failure, fear of death, fear of fire, fear of the loss of children or you are all basic fears. As the head of household, I must be the one who is not afraid and support you. Explaining my fears is the hardest to share with you. I feel fear in telling you of fear because you will not be able to use me as a support for your fears.

"Remember the two accidents we saw on the road the other day, fire trucks and ambulances and the woman with the baby in her arms? That night I had a dream we were hit from behind and the car caught fire. The gas tank split and all I could see was me trying to get Shari out of the car seat. I saw it over and over again. The next morning, I thought about it while driving to work. I never saw the end of the dream and I do not know if I got her out all right, I just drove to work with a sick feeling in my stomach. I guess if this is a measure of love, I love all of you very much. I need you all as we are a complete unit, each of us apart of the other and I fear losing you...."

The process of revealing this to Linda was so hard it was almost unbearable. It took all the strength and guts and the confidence I had to put this into a reflection. I felt confused as to whether or not this was really me.

At this point in the weekend, we give the couples the question for reflection and dialogue.

When they return to the conference room, we share one more story and then suggest an open-ended dialogue. We asked them to write in their individual rooms and then to discuss their feelings until they feel they have made progress in understanding. The story we relate:

There Are Two Seas

There are two seas in the land of Israel. One is fresh and fish are in it, splashes of green adorn its banks. Trees spread their branches over it and stretch out their thirsty roots to sip its healing waters. Along its shore, children play. The River Jordan creates this sea with sparkling water it receives from the hills.

The River Jordan flows on south to another sea. Here there is no splash of fish, no fluttering leaf, no song of birds, and no children's laughter. Travelers choose another route unless on urgent business. The air hangs heavy above its waters. Neither beast nor fowl will drink its waters.

What makes this mighty difference in these seas? The River Jordan empties the same good water into both. Not the soil in which they lie, not the country roundabout.

This is the difference the Sea of Galilee receives but does not keep the Jordan. For every drop that flows into it, another drop flows out. The giving and receiving share in equal measure.

The other sea is shrewder; it hordes its income jealously. It will not be tempted into any generous impulse. Every drop it gets, it keeps.

The Sea of Galilee gives and lives. The other sea gives nothing; it is called the Dead Sea.

There are two kinds of people in the world.

There are two seas in the land of Israel.

The couples are then asked to share what they have discovered about their relationship this weekend.

The verbal sharing of their thoughts and feelings goes on for a short but limited period.

We then explained that open dialogue is without time limit. We asked them to dig deep and try to feel their spouses' feelings. We also suggest this might be a suitable time to share their "encounter with self" with each other.

The last question for the night:

What feelings do I have today that I cannot or will not share with you, and how does it make me feel?

Chapter 7
The "We, God, and Community" Phase of the Weekend Sanctification

This presentation occurs at 8:15 A.M. on Monday morning. The couples now have begun to understand and appreciate the whole concept of the weekend. Closeness and newly found love is obvious by the demeanor of the weekend. The couples are hardly discussing the real world anymore and have become attuned to each other. Those who wanted to have attended a morning service and have enjoyed breakfast.

The purpose of this talk is to introduce the Judaic concept of married life. It is designed to make them more aware that the sanctification of their marital relationship called Kiddushin (small sanctuary) is not imposed on them from the outside, but that it grows between them and upon them in the manner in which they live their relationship. Marriage is a Mitzvah (blessing) and activity ordained by God. The degree to which each couple fulfils that Mitzvah is sanctified.

The goal of this talk is to inspire them for the greatest effort in their life, to fulfill their commitment to each other. It also explains that the Jewish community has a stake in their marital relationship.

This presentation draws on the other talks, especially Encounter with Self, Marriage in the Modern World, Marriage and the Plan of God, and Confidence and Dialogue, and it demands an understanding of the dialogue technique, which has been explained in all the other talks. The specific purpose of this talk is to prepare them for the matrimonial evaluation that follows this presentation. It is designed to develop their awareness of how important they are as a couple. It is to help them fall in love all over again with one another. It is also to give them an overview: to get away from the idea that they are just another married couple, and it really is not particularly important except to themselves. It is to help them recognize and begin a commitment toward creating a difference between living marriage and state of matrimony, realizing the awesomeness and beauty of their marital relationship. This the core presentation of the Encounter Weekend. It is the basis of their struggle in Matrimonial Spirituality to reevaluate their jobs, home, and relationship with their children. It is the foundation for their need to immerse in a new way of life.

On our original weekend, this presentation was called "The Sacrament and Its Graces." The concept is like sanctification. It asks us to share our attitudes toward marriage on our wedding day and our attitudes toward our marriage after Marriage Encounter. In Catholicism the marriage is considered a Sacrament. A Sacrament is not less that than other Sacraments that are instituted by Christ ...that it is as holy as the priesthood, that it is truly a sign of Christ's loves as the Eucharist, that it is much a way of witnessing Catholics' belief in their choice of God as are the Sacraments of Baptism and Confirmation. It defined Grace as a specific capability to love. Grace is a gift, and like all gifts it makes something possible. Grace accompanies the other Sacraments, like the Sacrament of Matrimony.

For us, it meant reinterpreting this to fit our religious outlook and to combine our love feelings with the meaning of a Sacrament to us.

A Sacramental Way of Life
What Does It Mean?

- It means that we must be open to God's plan for us and for our relation to the world.
- It means that we must be willing to question every action, every judgment, every value, every assumption about our day-to-day living—to see

whether it allows our love to grow or whether it diminishes us and our relationship to others.

- It means we attempt to make our home a small Sanctuary (mikdosh-miat).
- It means that we are bound to all those who believe the things we do, to our Church, the community of believers we share our faith with, and that we recognize an obligation and responsibility to them and to their need for us as well as our need for them.
- It means that we have a unique contribution to make to the world, and that the world will be less if we do not make it, and if we do make that contribution the world will be the place God intended it to be.
- It means that we can no longer afford to indulge in a poor self-image, but our own specialness and our own goodness should be so apparent to us that we see our vocation in life as one of sharing ourselves with others.
- It means that we, as lovers, recognize ourselves as different than what the world wants us to be, and that we be prepared to recognize and endure what that difference means.
- It means that we will have to continually struggle to make this vision come alive, but it also means that we will know joy that we did not think possible.
- It means that we must begin today.
- It means that we must live it each day.
- It means that we must choose to not Dialogue and die but to Dialogue and live.

This presentation is used to introduce the longest period of reflection and dialogue for the entire weekend. This is the 90/90 dialogue. The couples are told this refection and dialogue is the columniation of their encounter experience.

They will have 90 minutes to write and 90 minutes to dialogue on the question of a handout, which follows and is given to the couples before they begin writing. The handout follows:

AND THOU SHALT LOVE

MATRIMONIAL EVALUATION

1. WHAT ARE MY REASONS FOR WANTING TO GO ON LIVING?

2. WHAT ARE MY REASONS FOR WANTING TO GO ON LIVING WITH YOU?

3. WHAT ARE THE QUALITIES WHICH MOST ATTRACTED ME TO YOU?

4. I FEEL I NEED YOUR HELP SPECIFICALLY IN________________.

5. DO I SEE AND ACCEPT YOU AS YOU REALLY ARE? EXPLAIN FULLY IN LOVING DETAIL.

6. DO YOU SEE AND ACCEPT ME AS I REALLY AM? EXPLAIN FULLY IN LOVING DETAIL.

7. WHAT ARE MY FEELINGS ABOUT OUR SEXUAL RELATIONS?

8. WHAT ARE MY FEELINGS ABOUT G-D'S COMMITTMENT TO OUR MARRIAGE?

Music is introduced here with a scene from *Man of La Mancha* to each his dulcinea and to dream the impossible dream (to be discussed later).

After the 90/90

After the 90-minute reflection and 90-minute dialogue, the couples are brought from their rooms as a group when the team couples walk through the halls with music playing. Those couples who have made as good encounter join them in the halls with the other couples. Once they return to the conference room, additional music is played and the couple have an opportunity to bask in the results of their encounter experience.

A short presentation is given about the cost of the weekend, and a request is made for each couple to assess the value of the weekend and pay as little or as much as they choose. They are given a blank envelope and told not to put their names on it but to choose an amount the weekend is worth to them and deposit it into the envelope.

Chapter 8
Matrimonial Spirituality

*T*his presentation is given at about 11:30 A.M. on Monday morning. It occurs after the 90-90 and after the financial talk.

The purpose of this presentation is to point out that God's plan is to be a couple and that they must reevaluate their decisions, goals, plans about job, house, and children. Not because their choices are bad, but because they have a different awareness now. This talk is about the other half of the Marriage Encounter experience, the ongoing effort to maintain open communication with each other. The effort to live out God's plan for their marriage. It summarizes all that has gone before. It is the practical part spelling out the couple's goals in living God's plan.

It is to show them that their spirituality is not just belonging to one another, it is not just a series of actions. The ideas it illustrates is that their relationship comes first before everything else, that their other responsibilities and relationships must be an outgrowth of and as an expression of their relationship to one another. The presentation strives for a total commitment to the daily 10&10 as a way to keep alive their commitment to make their relationship first.

The question following this presentation is: How does my commitment to our daily 10&10 make me feel? What are my feelings about our daily 10&10?

On our original weekend, I answered these questions as follows:

"Dear Linda,

I feel some good feelings about the 10&10 which I have to tell you. I hope you understand them as well as you understand me because some of them are not good, and I need your loving help in getting me to accept them.

"My First feeling is one of apprehension I know the daily 10 and 10 isn't going to take a lot of time, but it really represents a big commitment. I feel unsure about my ability to carry it out fully although I want to. I worry about committing myself to you and possibly letting you down. How about when I'm away from home, I know we will miss it terribly because I will really miss you more. This weekend is going to change our lives. The love we have replenished is going to grow deeper and stronger. We will want more dialogue and I fear I will not be able to do it. Maybe I am overviewing the entire situation. I feel good knowing your love for me and I want to keep this up. In the past I may have committed myself to something and made you promises only to break them shortly thereafter. I know now that our love is so strong, I can't do this without it being full and total..."

On our original weekend, Linda answered this question as follows:

"My commitment to the 10 &10 makes me feel wonderful because it will be a continuation and strengthening of our great love that started this weekend. I am looking forward to it because it will help us to understand and grow together. I will know you better and the more I know you, the more I love you. Besides helping our marriage, it will help me realize my true feelings. When I first started writing reflections, I added endearing terms because I thought they

would make you feel good. But as I wrote it, I meant it more and it was much easier to discover my true feelings. It will be a quiet time every day for just you and me. It will be a few real moments out of the otherwise artificial world. It will give us the inner strength to carry us through the next 23 and ½ hours. It will also be our time to renew our love feelings and do the only important thing in the world, share our love. Right now, the only way I have for really expressing my feelings to you is through reflection, very much more than dialogue. My commitment to the daily 10 and 10 is my salvation I feel my strongest emotions when I am writing you a love letter…."

We did commit to our daily 10&10 and continued it for about eight years. It profoundly changed our lives.

The Open and Jewish Couple
This talk is given about 2:00 P.M. on Monday afternoon. It takes place right after lunch, when the couples have completed their financial contribution to the weekend.

The purpose of this talk is to let the couples know that their love is intimate, but not private. They must be made aware that their love must be shared for it to continue to grow. As a Jewish loving couple, they have a stake in and an obligation to the community generally and the Jewish community in particular. The couples are made aware that they have increased power (influence and impact) as a loving couple.

Rabbi Hillel said, "If I am not for myself who will be for me? If I am for myself alone, what am I, and if not now, when?" This is the clarion call of the Jewish tradition to the importance of involvement in the Jewish community.

On our original weekend, this presentation was called "The Open and Apostolic Couple." We had received letters from other couples in the community saying they were praying for the success of our weekend. The team couple giving this talk spoke about becoming an apostolic couple and sharing our love with the balance of the community. They said we cannot continue the dialogue concept unless we became part of a community sharing similar thoughts and experiences. The Catholic Church made it clear that Marriage Encounter was an experience that thrived on shared communication and commitment. It required continuation of commitment to fulfil the requirements of the Sacrament.

For Linda and me, this meant converting the words to an application to our Faith. We had experienced a great awakening in our marriage and relationship and understood the need for us to become part of a community where reflection and dialogue was continued and reinforced.

The quote "Love in your heart wasn't put there to stay, Love isn't love till you give it away" was emphasized by the presenting couple.

The question asked of us was: "In what specific ways are we going to share our couple love?"

Linda responded:

"Hi Cookie:

"We're going to be honest and open with each other. We're going to share our love and deepest feelings. We're going to be able to express our feeling without being hurt or fear of rejection. We're going to work at our commitment to the daily 10 and 10 and not quit when the going gets rough and we're going to realize that nothing comes easy and work at it as hard as work at our separate jobs.

"We're going to stay active with Encounter activities because they have a purpose and will help us when need it. We will try as hard as we can not to be married singles and we're not going to force our love on each other or other people…."

I added:

"As strongly as you felt and made me feel about the 10&10 that's how strongly I feel about carrying Marriage Encounter on. My motivation is threefold, first we will of course follow through and give our profound love to our kids. They are in the formative years of their lives and our love will mean much to them. Our continued 10&10 will help us. Secondly, we should spread our love to our family and friends. They will see us as Len and Gerry mentioned saw what true love can do and has done for us. It is so strong, it can do anything. Finally I would love to make a commitment to our religion. It is so fortunate we are not like some people we know, and that our minds are open.

"We have done a great thing by attending this weekend. Let's spread it to our fellow Jews so they can have the love we found in this retreat house. Work with me and we will always be as close as we are today."

This was the last presentation for the weekend.

The weekend concluded with a renewal of marriage vows, a blessing of the Dialogue Books, and a verbal sharing of what the weekend meant to each couple. By the end of the sharing period, there was a rededication to our relationship and a wish for Godspeed for all who were going home to their families.

Chapter 9
The Music of Marriage Encounter

The use of music is a very important part of the Marriage Encounter experience. *Man of La Mancha* is the music that was used frequently during the Marriage Encounter Weekend. It is currently unknown if it is still in use today. From our perspective, the use of this show music greatly enhanced our experience.

Music creates a memory in the brain, which allows us to recall the experience and memory that was associated with the time when the music was first heard. In the Marriage Encounter Weekend, we are striving for openness with our feelings. The entire weekend is an experience where our feelings and emotions are being exposed. As result, the deep sense of emotions is at the surface. The music used on the weekend along with handouts allow us to go back and vividly recall the weekend experience.

Today, hearing any of the songs from the weekend renews our feelings for each other and reinforces all that we learned on the weekend many years ago.

For example, in the presentation of encounter with self we are exposed to the song "Aldonza" from the *La Mancha* show, which is used to illustrate the poor self-image as quoted in the following insert.

ALDONZA

AND THOU SHALT LOVE

"My Lady!...I'm not your lady; I'm not any kind of a lady".

"I was spawned in a ditch by a mother who left me there, naked and cold and too hungry to cry. I never blamed her. I'm sure she left hoping that I'd have the good sense to die.

Then, of course, there's my father; I'm told that young ladies can point to their fathers with maidenly pride; mine was a regiment here for an hour-- I can't even tell you which tide".

So, of course, I became as befitted my delicate birth--the most casual bride of the murdering scum of the earth...
                    and still he torments me!

How should I be a "lady"?

For a "lady" has modest and maidenly airs and a virture I somehow suspect that I lack. It's hard to remember these maidenly airs in a stable laid flat on your back.

Won't you look at me, look at me, God, won't you look at me! look at the kitchen-slut reeking with sweat--born on a dungheap to die on a dungheap, a strumpet men use and forget......

If you feel that you see me not quite at my virginal best, cross my palm with a coin and I'll willingly show you the rest...

Take the clouds from your eyes and see me as I really am.

You have shown me the sky, but what good is the sky to a creature who never knew better than crawl--of all the cruel devils who badgered and battered me, you are the cruelest of all!

Can't you see what your gentle insanities do to me, rob me of anger and give me despair? Blows and abuse I can take and give back again--tenderness I cannot bear.

So don't reach out to me when your sweet "Dulcinea" you call--

I am only a boozer...I know that I am nothing at all!"

Additional songs from the show are used just befoire the 90/90 long dialogue to illiustrate the depth to which Aldonza had changed and grown. After the death scene song is played, "The Impossible Dream" is used to launch a long reflection and dialogue period. It is designed to send the couples to really open their hearts to each other. The "Dolcenia Death Scene" handout follows:

AND THOU SHALT LOVE

```
"Please...try to remember--you looked at me and called by
another name...Dulcinea, Dulcinea--once you found a girl and
called her "Dulcinea"

When you spoke the name, an angel seemed to whisper, "Dulcinea,
Dulcinea"

Dulcinea, Dulcinea...Won't you please bring back the dream of
Dulcinea?
Won't you please give back the bright and shining glory of
"Dulcinea, Dulcinea"?

"Perhaps..perhaps it was not a dream---"

"You spoke of a dream...    about the 'quest'...?

"The quest...the words...tell me, tell me the words..."

"To dream the impossible dream...but they're your own words...

to fight the unbeatable foe...Don't you remember?

to bear with unbearable sorrow--you must remember!

to run where the brave dare not go"

"To right the unrightable wrong...to love pure and chaste from afar..

to try when your arms are too weary to reach the unreachable star..!"

"Thank you, my Lord!"-- "But this is unseemly, my lady,-- on thy
knees to me!

"My Lord, you're not well! -- "Not well?  What is illness to the
body of a knight - errant?? What matter wounds??for each time
she falls she shall rise again!! and woe to the wicked!!

"Sancho!" -- Here, your grace,"-- "my armor, my sword!

"More misadventure??"--"Adventure, too, friend,.."... for the
trumpets of glory now call me to ride, yes, the trumpets are
calling to me -- and wherever I ride, ever Sancho at my side, my
squire and my lady shall be -- I am I, Don Quizote, the Lord of
La Mancha our destiny calls and recalls - and the wild winds of
fortune shall carry us onward...whithersoever they blow -- onward
to glory I..go'.
```

After the 90-90, the couples are gathered from their rooms hearing the sounds of music. The team couples walk through and play the songs "We've Only Just Begun," made peopular by the Carpenters; "I'd Like to Teach the World to Sing," recorded by the New Seekers; The Marriage Encounter Theme Song ("I'll Never Find Another You"; "There Is a New

World Somewhere," recorded by the New Seekers; the Wedding Song, made popular by Paul Stukey; and "What the World Needs Now Is Love," recorded by Dionne Warwick. As the couples return to the conference room, additional music is played.

AND THOU SHALT LOVE   The Coke Song

          I'd like to build the world a home and furnish it with love,
           Grow apple trees and honey bees, and snow white turtle doves.
          I'd like to teach the world to sing in perfect harmony, I'd like
           to hold it in my arms and keep it company.
          It's the real thing, what the world wants today, that's the way
           it will stay, it's the real thing.

                    There's A New World Somewhere
     There's a new world somewhere, they call the Promised land;
       And I'll be there someday, if you will hold my hand;
     I still need you there beside me, no matter what I do;
       For I know I'll never find another you.

     There is always someone for each of us they say,
       And you'll be my someone forever and a day;
     I could search the whole world over, until my life is through,
       And I know I'll never find another you.
     It's a long, long, journey, so stay by my side,
       If I walk through a storm you'll be my guide, my guide...

     If they gave me a fortune my treasure would be small,
       I could lose it all tomoroww and never mind at all!
     But if I should lose your love dear, I don't know what I'd do,
       For I know I'll never find another you.

                    I Can't Give You Anything But Love
          I can't give you anything but love, baby,
            That's the only thing I've plenty of, baby.
          Dream awhile, scheme awhile, you're sure to find
            Happiness, and I guess, all the things you've always pined for.
          Gee, I'd like to see you looking swell, baby,
            Diamond bracelets Woolworth's doesn't sell, baby.
          Til that lucky day I know darn well, baby.
            I can't give you anthing but love.

                    It Had to be You
          It had to be you, it had to be you; I wandered around,
            and finally found somebody who,
          Could make me be blue, could make me be true;
            And even be glad, just to be sad, thinking of you.

          Some others I've seen, might never be mean, might never be
            cross, might never be boss, but they wouldn't do
          For nobody else gave me that thrill, with all your faults
            I love you still
          It had to be you, wonderful you, it had to be you.

Chapter 10
Epilogue

After the original Marriage Encounter Weekend, Linda and I did follow through with our commitment to the daily 10&10. We dialogued daily for the next eight years, and we grew and grew in our couple relationship. We returned to the modern world with a different attitude.

I quit many single activities like the Knights of Pythias and the Civil Defense and Disaster Squad.

We devoted much of our time to our encounter community, through renewals, anniversary weekends, rap groups, and a local community image group, where we shared our struggle with dialogue and made a whole new group of friends.

As was earlier stated, we were asked to make an Encounter Weekend for team training. After our training, we prepared for and led 22 Marriage Encounter Weekends.

We also accepted the job of helping other couples become teams in the Jewish Expression of Marriage Encounter, as the lead administrative couple for the state of New Jersey.

We also were blessed to spread our couple love across the country. We led weekends in Toledo, Ohio; Charlotte, North Carolina; Minneapolis, Minnesota; and Los Angeles, California, as well as New York and New Jersey.

We also attended a very religious-oriented Encounter Weekend with an orthodox rabbinic couple as well as an Encounter Weekend with our teenage children.

We continued to dialogue together and filled many books with reflections.

After about eight years we became less involved in community activities by our own choice. We continued our 10&10, though not as frequently.

In March of 2023 will celebrate our 59th anniversary. We are still as much in love as when we first made our Encounter Weekend. Our children are happily married, each for 27 years. We are blessed with five grandchildren, all well adjusted and very happy.

Marriage Encounter has greatly influenced our lives and we feel contributed to us having a very happy marriage, a wonderful family, and our longevity. We thank our friends Tom and Sandy Cherubini for sending us on the most wonderful experience of our lives.